THE MISTY LETTERS

FACTS KIDS WISH YOU KNEW ABOUT DYSLEXIA

"Tell me and I forget.

Teach me and I learn.

Involve me and I remember."

- Benjamin Franklin

PREAMBLE

Imagine having important needs and ideas to communicate, but being unable to express them. Perhaps feeling bombarded by sights and sounds, unable to focus your attention. Or trying to read or add but not being able to make sense of the letters or numbers. You may not need to imagine. You may be the parent, guardian or teacher of a child experiencing academic problems, or have someone in your family diagnosed as learning disabled, or, possibly as a child you were told you had a reading problem called dyslexia or some other learning handicap.

Although different from person to person, these difficulties make up the common daily experiences of many learning disabled children, adolescents, and adults. A person with a learning disability may experience a cycle of academic failure and lowered self-esteem. Having these handicaps or living with someone who has them can bring overwhelming frustration.

But the prospects are hopeful. It is important to remember that a person with a learning disability can learn. The disability usually only affects certain limited areas of a child's development. In fact, rarely are learning disabilities severe enough to impair a person's potential to live a happy, normal and successful life.

This book provides an understanding on how kids with learning disabilities feel and what you as a parent, guardian or teacher can expect. This is an effort to provide information and support. Among these sources are, special education teachers, and mental health professionals who have helped identify and put in place the various symptoms of learning disabilities.

We are the human beings of 21st century. We live in the world of modernization, urbanization, industrialization, globalization, and above all the world of "Perfection & Cut throat, competition".

We want to strike for perfection in anything and everything we do! Being a part of an ever-growing and maddening rat race, we want to be ahead of the other constantly trying to excel. Now we do not really care if the person we are competing against is a sibling, a friend, an unknown person, a fellow student or a co-worker! Materializing has become the cutline and religion of modern civilization, and we apply it either consciously or unconsciously in every sphere of our life.

We have all now become mechanically timed robots living in concrete jungles where we repeatedly tell each other and ourselves that 24hours in a day is just not enough! Strike an ode to our controversial mechanical life's we just have to notice that parents today have totally lost the essence of parenting and happiness!

We have let ourselves into the Bermuda triangle of "Beat the Time" that the general concept of reading to your child has been forgotten! Mundane things that can bring joy into the family or put a smile on the child's face are being forgotten and left untapped!

Faults, mistakes, errors have become a taboo these days! Perfection is what we are seeking and yet again in our struggle for perfection we are forgetting that too much perfection isn't beautiful, and we have just lost the natural beauty and its true natural individuality.

Today we as parents cannot tolerate the fact that our kids are not perfect! We – the so called modern and educated perfect parents of this perfect world, need to realize that when it comes to molding our children it is cultivating the desire to excel and be happy that matters and not just blindly run the rat race! Five out of ten parents keep hauling & complaining that their child does not do this, does not do that, is so irresponsible, mischievous, ill-mannered and the list is just never ending!

Parents who have a constant sense of threat in them tend to get irritated and frustrated with themselves and end up saying that the kids are just little too much for them to handle! For them children are not "Little angles" or "bundles of joy"! Jawaharlal Nehru's statement "Children are my god!" When punctuated the right way the meaning comes out strong! Similarly when punctuated the wrong way.....the meaning comes out stronger! Parents today have started to say "children are, MY GOD!!!!"

Children have now become a piece of asset! The more you invest on them better are the profits and advantages! COMPARISION! Why compare one individual with another? A child is an individual with likes and dislikes, individuality and a sense of self-esteem! Not trying to say that comparison is bad but the manner in which it is done should be reconsidered by parents as it does have a deep and long-term effect on the children. The when, how, where and what logistics should be considered! Parents should realize and resolve issues or concerns rather than just plain compare! COMPARISION should have a positive effect on the child!

Peer pressure, stress and constant competition directed towards the child by the parents, teachers, family and the competitive society stress's the child out beyond ones wild imagination! Every child needs to talk to someone to whom he or she can open his or her heart out and speak fearlessly and frankly about their designs, dreams, aspirations, problems and agonies.

To keep up to the parents expectation and to establish themselves in the society as Engineers, Doctors, MBBS etc; a child is burdened with a load of educational pressure with the increase in case of child delinquencies or crime suicidal attempts among students, the world Heart Organization (WHO) made commendation of mandatory counseling on a regular basis in each and every school.

Section 1:

Learning Disabilities...

Let's classify them!

"Learning disability" is not a diagnosis that can be done or related to like other physical ailments. Physical ailments imply a single, known cause with a predictable set of symptoms. LD is a broad term that covers a pool of possible causes, symptoms, treatments, and outcomes. Partly because learning disabilities can show up in so many forms, it is difficult to diagnose or to pinpoint the causes. And no one knows of an oral medication or remedy that will cure them.

Not all learning problems are necessarily learning disabilities. Many children are simply slower in developing certain skills. Because children show natural differences in their rate of development, sometimes what seems to be a learning disability may simply be a delay in maturity! To be diagnosed as a learning disability, specific criteria must be met.

The criteria and characteristics for diagnosing learning disabilities appear in a reference book called the DSM (short for the Diagnostic and Statistical Manual of Mental Disorders). The DSM diagnosis is commonly used when applying for health insurance coverage of diagnostic and treatment services.

Researchers and practitioners divide learning disability into:

- Developmental speech and language disorders
- Academic skills disorders

DEVELOPMENTAL SPEECH AND LANGUAGE DISORDERS:

Speech and language problems are often the earliest indicators of a learning disability. People with developmental speech and language disorders have difficulty producing speech sounds, using spoken language to communicate, or understanding what other people say. Depending on the problem, the specific classifications are:

- Developmental articulation disorder
- Developmental expressive language disorder
- Developmental receptive language disorder

DEVELOPMENTAL ARTICULATION DISORDER:

Children with this disorder may have trouble controlling their rate of speech. Or they may lag behind playmates in learning to make speech sounds. For example, you could come around kids who would say "wabbit" instead of "rabbit" and "thwim" for "swim." Or say "bled" for "bread." Researchers say developmental articulation disorders are common. They appear in at least 10% of children younger than age 8. Fortunately, articulation disorders can often be outgrown or successfully treated with speech therapy and many times naturally get corrected.

DEVELOPMENTAL EXPRESSIVE LANGUAGE DISORDER:

Some children with language impairments have problems expressing themselves in speech. Their disorder is called, therefore, a developmental expressive language disorder.

Expressive language disorder can take other forms. A 4-year-old who speaks only in two-word phrases and a 6-year-old who can't answer simple questions can be termed as one with expressive language disability.

DEVELOPMENTAL RECEPTIVE LANGUAGE DISORDER:

Some kids have trouble understanding certain aspects of speech. It's as if their brains are set to a different frequency and the reception is poor. There's the toddler who doesn't respond to his name, a pre-schooler who hands you a ball when you asked for a bell, or a child who consistently can't follow simple directions. Their hearing is fine, but they can't make sense of certain sounds, words, or sentences they hear. They may even seem inattentive. Mental practitioners say these people have a receptive language disorder. Because using and understanding speech are strongly related, many people with receptive language disorders also have an expressive language disability. Of course, in kids, some misuse of sounds, words, or grammar is a normal part of learning to speak. It's only when these problems persist that there is any cause for concern.

ACADEMIC SKILLS DISORDERS:

Students with academic skills disorders are often years behind their classmates in developing reading, writing, or arithmetic skills. The diagnoses in this category include:

- Developmental reading disorder
- Developmental writing disorder
- Developmental arithmetic disorder

Developmental Reading Disorder:

This type of disorder, also known as dyslexia, is quite widespread. In fact, reading disabilities affect 2 to 8 percent of elementary school children say researchers. Considering that to read, you must simultaneously be able to:

- Focus attention on the printed marks and control eye movements across the page
- Recognize the sounds associated with letters
- Understand words and grammar
- Build ideas and images
- Compare new ideas to what you already know
- Store ideas in memory

These activities that sound so simple and easy to us in real require a strong network of nerve cells that connect the brain's centres of vision, language, and memory.

A person can have problems in any of the tasks involved in reading. However, researchers found that a significant number of people with dyslexia share an inability to distinguish or separate the sounds in spoken words. Kids can't identify a word by the phonetic sound of the individual letter. Other children with dyslexia may have trouble with rhyming games, such as rhyming "rat" with "cat." Yet researchers have found these skills as fundamentals to read or learn.

There is more to reading than recognizing words. When the brain is unable to form images or relate new ideas to those stored in memory, the reader can't understand or remember the new concepts. So other types of reading disabilities can appear in the children as they grow older as focus of reading shifts from word identification to comprehension.

Developmental Writing Disorder:

 Writing, too, involves several brain areas and functions. The brain networks for vocabulary, grammar, hand movement, and memory must all be in good working order. So a developmental writing disorder may result from problems in any of these areas. Children, who are unable to distinguish the sequence of sounds in a word, have problems with spelling. A child with a writing disability might be unable to compose complete, grammatical sentences.

Developmental Arithmetic Disorder:

If you doubt that arithmetic is a complex process, think of the steps you take to solve this simple problem: 25 divided by 3 equals?
Arithmetic involves recognizing numbers and symbols, memorizing facts such as the multiplication table, aligning numbers, and understanding abstract concepts like place value and fractions.

Any of these may be difficult for children with developmental arithmetic disorders. Problems with numbers or basic concepts are likely to show up early. Disabilities that appear in the later grades are more often tied to problems in reasoning.

As a child I remember not being able to perform simple arithmetic problems. So much so that memorising tables proved useless cause I could never bear them in my memory, and slowly I developed a feeling that I remember later classifying as "aversion" towards numbers. It's funny how even today I hear myself saying "Do not talk numbers to me! My brain shuts-off!!"

Many aspects of speaking, listening, reading, writing, and arithmetic overlap and build on the same brain capabilities. So it's not surprising that people can be diagnosed as having more than one area of learning disability. For example, the ability to understand language underlies learning to speak.

Therefore, any disorder that hinders the ability to understand language will also interfere with the development of speech, which in turn hinders learning to read and write. A single gap in the brain's operation can disrupt many types of activity.

Attention Disorders:

Nearly 20% of children in a classroom have issues that teachers relate as "unable to focus their attention."

Some children and adults who have attention disorders appear to daydream excessively. And once you get their attention, they're often easily distracted. Children tend to mentally drift off into a world of their own. Children with Attention Disorders may have a number of learning difficulties. Some children, who tend to be quite, have their problems go unnoticed. They may be passed along from grade to grade, without getting the special assistance they need.

In a large proportion of affected children--mostly boys--the attention deficit is accompanied by hyperactivity, destructive and violent. A child with attention deficit hyperactivity disorder—ADHD act impulsively, running into traffic or toppling desks. Young kids, jump on the bed till exhausted. They blurt out answers and interrupt. In games, they can't wait their turn.
Because of their constant motion and explosive energy, hyperactive children often get into trouble with parents, teachers, and peers.

By adolescence, physical hyperactivity usually subsides into fidgeting and restlessness. But the problems with attention and concentration often continue into adulthood. At work, adults with ADHD often have trouble organizing tasks or completing their work. They don't seem to listen to or follow directions. Their work may be messy and appear careless.

Attention disorders, with or without hyperactivity, are not considered learning disabilities in themselves. However, because attention problems can seriously interfere with school performance, they often accompany academic skills disorders.

When we talk about learning and the difficulty to learn, there are many factors that are usually on the prime access. Mostly people consider that it is laziness or the sheer indifference that the child or the individual is showing towards education. Seldom do you come across parents who are ready to accept that the issue might be something different.

Dyslexic relatedness to how the brain functions is complicated. Researchers have been contemplating and analysing the topic ever since dyslexia was spoken about a hundred years ago.

W. Pringle Morgan (cited in Shaywitz, 1996), a doctor in Sussex, England, described the puzzling case of a boy in the British Medical Journal: "Percy ... aged 14 ... has always been a bright and intelligent boy, quick at games, and in no way inferior to others of his age. His great difficulty has been – and is now – his inability to read"

Almost every teacher I have spoken to has at least one student who could fit the same description written so many years ago. This situation leads many teachers and parents to wonder why their articulate, clearly bright student has so many problems with what appears to be a simple task – 'READING' something that seems easily administrable to others.

Having information about the likely explanation for and the potential cause of the child's difficulties often relieves parents/teachers' fears and uncertainties about how to teach the child and how to think about providing instructions that are relevant and effective. Current research on dyslexia and the brain provide the most up-to-date information available about the problems faced by over 2.8 million school-aged children.

When talking with teachers about their students who struggle with reading, I have encountered similar types of questions from teachers. They often wonder, What is dyslexia? What does brain research tell us about reading problems and what does this information mean for classroom instruction?

The purpose of this book is to explain the answers to these questions and provide foundational knowledge that will lead to a firmer understanding of the underlying characteristics of children with dyslexia. A greater understanding of the current brain research and how it relates to students with dyslexia is important in education and will help teachers understand and evaluate possible instructional interventions to help their students succeed in the classroom

Section 2:

BREAKING THE ICE WITH THE REALISATION

I am the last person anyone would go to for information about dyslexia. I grew up as the classic bookworm. My goal was to read every book in my library, and, from the piles of books I checked out each week, one would think that I might have succeeded!   Reading was my pleasure (and even my guilty pleasure, when it was after my bedtime). By that point, my book-a-day habit was long established.

Now fast-forward twenty years: I am a new mother, starting excitedly to read to and with my two young children. We began with old classics, and quickly discovered new favourite authors as well. Good night meant me reading to my kids. My son especially liked to be read to, and paid rapt attention.

Within a few years, however, it was clear that my son did not share my love of reading. While he enjoyed being read to, reading was something that had to be externally imposed. This usually resulted in howling, cribbing, getting cranky and finally me giving up!!!??

My son, like many younger children, learned many things by osmosis, while my daughter was mastering them. By then
their school taught reading using the picture spot technique, and his decoding skills far exceeded his sisters.

His grades were good, and everyone at school loved him. He could and still does make everybody laugh. Witty, humorous, poker faced, intelligent, analytical, curious for details, never accepts instructions unless told why he has to do it the way he is being asked to.

He sometimes would come home saying things like "I'm the dumbest person in my class". It was a class full of very bright kids of achievement-oriented parents! So I always just reassured him that wasn't true. He was a poor tester, especially on standardized tests that involved writing! So what did I do? I thought it was laziness coupled with anxiety issues.

He never read for pleasure, though, and even tuned away when others were reading aloud. Trouble in school started immediately after the first term examinations of Lower Kindergarten. Teachers thought he was just plain playful. Needs more time to dwell into the educational system!

Then trotted along Upper Kindergarten!!! I felt they were just preparing him for the horrendous life in school where he had to toil and toil and toil and toil more. I heard him ask, "If the phonetic sound for Cat sounds like K why is it not KAT but CAT??" I saw him looking wide eyed at me and heard him ask "Ma! Am I going to be this different all the time?"

I felt a part of me break. I end up calling my mom and crying to her. Well, I had nowhere else to go!! So I thought! I started noticing his change in behaviour. Drawing comparisons between my daughter and him it started to dawn upon me that he was going low on confidence. My daughter always bubbly and energetic had loads of things to tell me about school. She would enter the doorway saying, "Ma! You know what happened in school today......" and the stories were never ending! When I turned around to ask him about school, he would shrug his shoulders and say it was fine, we dint do anything much!

A child who was confident, bright and enthusiastic, always ready to learn something new or try something new started to behave reluctant and indifferent! Parents' teachers meetings' were nothing but complains from their end and me trying to explain to them that he was a little different than the other kids but not a dumb child and just needed that extra care and attention!

One particularly damaging misunderstanding of the condition is the belief that students who suffer with dyslexia possess diminished academic potential. Many people, teachers included think that students who require adaptations and adjusted expectations related to reading speed, spelling accuracy and their mode of written expression must also necessitate adjusted intellectual expectations.

This is a big error. I consider Dyslexia as a mechanical disability, not a thinking disability. Teachers and parents need to communicate and understand this, and -- most of all -- dyslexic children need to know this. With specialized reading instruction and basic accommodations, dyslexic learners at any school can become engaged, high-performing students.

One day I pulled up my sock and said enough is enough I am not letting anyone break my child down emotionally! So I walked up to the school put down a request for a Transfer to another school.

Then started the journey, understanding how to simplify his life! Which meant, I had to start understanding patterns that followed him, or, patterns that he just could not get to shake away from him; I started categorising these patterns.

General symptoms, that occurred every day; I started to notice changes with his **Vision, Reading and Spelling** skills;

General:

- Appears bright, highly intelligent, and articulate but unable to read, write, or spell at grade level.
- Labeled lazy, dumb, careless, immature, "not trying hard enough," or "behavior problem."
- Isn't "behind enough" or "bad enough" to be helped in the school setting.
- High in IQ, yet may not test well academically; tests well orally, but not written.
- Feels dumb; has poor self-esteem; hides or covers up weaknesses with ingenious compensatory strategies; easily frustrated and emotional about school reading or testing.
- Talented in art, drama, music, sports, mechanics, story-telling, sales, business, designing, building, or engineering.
- Seems to "Zone out" or daydream often; gets lost easily or loses track of time.
- Difficulty sustaining attention; seems "hyper" or "daydreamer."
- Learns best through hands-on experience, demonstrations, experimentation, observation, and visual aids.

Vision, Reading, and Spelling:

- Complains of dizziness, headaches or stomach aches while reading.

- Confused by letters, numbers, words, sequences, or verbal explanations.
- Reading or writing shows repetitions, additions, transpositions, omissions, substitutions, and reversals in letters, numbers and/or words.
- Complains of feeling or seeing non-existent movement while reading, writing, or copying.
- Seems to have difficulty with vision, yet eye exams don't reveal a problem.
- Extremely keen sighted and observant, or lacks depth perception and peripheral vision.
- Reads and rereads with little comprehension.
- Spells phonetically and inconsistently.

Hearing and Speech:

- Has extended hearing; hears things not said or apparent to others; easily distracted by sounds.
- Difficulty putting thoughts into words; speaks in halting phrases; leaves sentences incomplete; stutters under stress; mispronounces long words, or transposes phrases, words, and syllables when speaking.

Writing and Motor Skills:

- Trouble with writing or copying; pencil grip is unusual; handwriting varies or is illegible.

- Clumsy, uncoordinated
- Difficulties with fine and/or gross motor skills and tasks; prone to motion-sickness.
- Can be ambidextrous, and often confuses left/right, over/under.

Math and Time Management:

- Has difficulty telling time, managing time, learning sequenced information or tasks, or being on time.
- Computing math shows dependence on finger counting and other tricks; knows answers, but can't do it on paper.
- Can count, but has difficulty counting objects and dealing with money.
- Can do arithmetic, but fails word problems; cannot grasp algebra or higher math.

Memory and Cognition:

- Excellent long-term memory for experiences, locations, and faces.
- Poor memory for sequences, facts and information that has not been experienced.
- Thinks primarily with images and feeling, not sounds or words (little internal dialogue).

Behaviour, Health, Development and Personality:

- Extremely disorderly or compulsively orderly.
- Can be class clown, trouble-maker, or too quiet.
- Had unusually early or late developmental stages (talking, crawling, walking, tying shoes).
- Prone to ear infections; sensitive to foods, additives, and chemical products.
- Can be an extra deep or light sleeper; bedwetting beyond appropriate age.
- Unusually high or low tolerance for pain.
- Strong sense of justice; emotionally sensitive; strives for perfection.
- Mistakes and symptoms increase dramatically with confusion, time pressure, emotional stress, or poor health.

How one learns to read and write is what classifies Dyslexia; or in terms of subtle differences in the way the brain responds to the written word. These differences make it more than usually difficult to learn to read, write and, sometimes, deal with numbers.

On the other side, it is proven and establishes that people with dyslexia are and can be more clear and advanced in their thought process and in the ways they see, understand and process nonverbal information. It is a proven fact that they are more creative and have solutions that are usually out of the box.

Dyslexia is a term that embraces them all. It is a complex situation that describes a difference in an individual's ability in processing information, performing tasks and activities and abilities which come into play when one needs to read and write. These processes and abilities are also likely to affect how one learns, organises a task and deals with many everyday tasks. One lives with dyslexia.

It is not a medical problem which can be cured nor does it make one a psychologically effected individual on the constant look out for psychiatric help or psychological assessment's. It's a genetic problem and lives with the individual, child or adult. It's important as parents or guardians that we help the person in understanding how to adapt and find new ways to deal with information processing, and getting around the original difficulties, and often exploiting their strengths to do this.

Kids with dyslexia are very thorough, because they leave nothing to chance. They plan carefully because they have to be prepared. Learning the fact that they have to work harder than other kids around them, develops the ability to focus and move on gradually but steadily in performing tasks.

They gradually overcome a lot of difficulties in acquiring skills which most kids learn to do automatically, or with ease.
You will more likely see them believe in their own ability to achieve their goals. Provided we as parents do not amplify this set back as hindrance or a probable step towards failure.

No child will have all the indicators. Many people will have several of the indicators. Some indicators are more common than others. The number of indicators observed does not indicate whether the dyslexia is mild, moderate or severe.

Everyone has strengths and weaknesses so people who do not have dyslexia will relate to a few of the signs. People who have dyslexia will tend to relate to a significant number of the following indicators.

Indicators of a possible learning difficulty arising from dyslexia in children:

- Difficulty with reading aloud.
- Difficulty with reading unfamiliar material.
- Tendency to mispronounce or misread words.
- Slow pace of reading.
- Reading for information only, not for pleasure.
- Understanding more easily when listening than when reading.
- Difficulty with spelling.
- Finding it hard to visualise words, or remember the sequence of letters in a word.
- Difficulty with sentence construction and punctuation.
- Difficulty putting information on paper.
- Difficulty in spotting mistakes made in written work.
- Finding it easier to express thoughts in words than in writing.
- Underachieving at school, particularly in exams.
- Having immature or ill formed handwriting.
- Tendency to be clumsy and uncoordinated.

- Confusing left and right.
- Finding it hard to remember things in sequence.
- Difficulty in remembering new information or new names.
- Synchronising multiple instructions.
- Getting phone messages wrong.
- Confusion with times and dates.
- Making silly mistakes.
- Randomly performing tasks.
- Poor short term memory. (Their long term memory is usually much more detailed)

How much dyslexia affects a child's life depends on many factors:

- The age at which the condition was diagnosed,
- The degree of severity,
- The ability of the individual,
- The type and quality of support received – both educational and social
- The personality of the individual.

Some people are lucky enough to have had their dyslexia identified as children and to have received support through their school years.

They have had an opportunity to understand their own learning difficulties and to take them into account when planning further education or choosing a career.

The fact that they have overcome basic literacy difficulties and even secured satisfactory results in examinations does not mean that they have been cured of their dyslexia. Information processing difficulties, poor short term memory, auditory processing deficits or hand-eye co-ordination difficulties do not go away.

Updating computer skills, learning to use new technology or new equipment, re-training which has to be undertaken in certain sectors of industry, can all be difficult for a person who thought that dyslexia was left behind with schooldays. If the difficulties encountered at school were severe, then as an adult they might have a reluctance to re-enter a learning situation.

Section 3:

What Causes Learning Disabilities?

Researchers indicate that dyslexia is caused by biological factors not emotional or family problems. Samuel Torrey Orton an American physician who pioneered the study of learning disabilities is best known for his work examining the causes and treatment of reading disability, or dyslexia. He was one among the first to describe the emotional aspects of dyslexia. According to his research, most of the dyslexic children in preschool are happy and well adjusted. Emotional problems begin to develop when early reading instruction fail to match their peer's style. Over the years, the frustration mounts as classmates surpass the dyslexic student in reading skills.

Recent research has identified many of the neurological and cognitive differences that contributes' to dyslexia. The vast majority of these factors appear due to genetic disorders than poor parenting or childhood depression or anxiety.

Understandably, one of the first questions parents ask when they learn their child has a learning disorder is "Why? What went wrong?"

Mental health professionals stress that since no one knows what causes learning disabilities, it doesn't help parents to look backward to search for possible reasons. Research shows that there are too many possibilities to pin down the cause of the disability with certainty. It is far more important for the family to move forward in finding ways to get help.

Researchers however, do need to study causes in an effort to identify ways to prevent learning disabilities.

Once, scientists thought that all learning disabilities were caused by a single neurological problem. But research supported by *National Institute of Mental Health* has helped us see that the causes are more diverse and complex. New evidence seems to show that most learning disabilities do not stem from a single, specific area of the brain, but from difficulties in bringing together information from various brain regions. Today, a leading theory is that learning disabilities stem from subtle disturbances in brain structures and functions. Some scientists believe that, in many cases, the disturbance begins before birth.

ERRORS IN FETAL BRAIN DEVELOPMENT:

Throughout pregnancy, the foetal brain develops from a few all-purpose cells into a complex organ made of billions of specialized, interconnected nerve cells called neurons. During this amazing evolution, things can go wrong that may alter how the neurons form or interconnect.

In the early stages of pregnancy, the brain stem forms. It controls basic life functions such as breathing and digestion. Later, a deep ridge divides the cerebrum--the thinking part of the brain--into two halves, a right and left hemisphere. Finally, the areas involved with processing sight, sound, and other senses develop, as well as the areas associated with attention, thinking, and emotion.

As new cells form, they move into place to create various brain structures. Nerve cells rapidly grow to form networks with other parts of the brain. These networks are what allow information to be shared among various regions of the brain.

Throughout pregnancy, this brain development is vulnerable to disruptions. If the disruption occurs early, the foetus may die, or the infant may be born with widespread disabilities and possibly mental retardation.

If the disruption occurs later, when the cells are becoming specialized and moving into place, it may leave errors in the cell makeup, location, or connections. Some researchers' believe that these errors may later show up as learning disorders.

OTHER FACTORS THAT AFFECT BRAIN DEVELOPMENT:

Through experiments with animals, scientists at *National Institute of Mental Health* and other research facilities are tracking clues to determine what disrupts brain development. By studying the normal processes of brain development, researchers can better understand what can go wrong.

Some of these studies are examining how genes, substance abuse, pregnancy problems, and toxins may affect the developing brain.

Genetic Factors:

The fact that learning disabilities tend to run in families indicates that there may be a genetic link. For example, children who lack some of the skills needed for reading, such as hearing the separate sounds of words, are likely to have a parent with a related problem. A parent's learning disability may take a slightly different form in the child. A parent who has a writing disorder may have a child with an expressive language disorder.

For this reason, it seems unlikely that specific learning disorders are inherited directly. Possibly, what is inherited is a subtle brain dysfunction that can in turn lead to a Learning Disability.

There may be an alternative explanation for why LD might seem to run in families. Some learning difficulties may actually stem from the family environment. For example, parents who have expressive language disorders might talk less to their children or the language they use may be distorted.

In such cases, the child lacks a good model for acquiring language and therefore, may seem to be learning disabled.

Tobacco, Alcohol, and Other Drug Use:

Many drugs taken by the mother pass directly to the foetus. Research shows that a mother's use of cigarettes, alcohol, or other drugs during pregnancy may have damaging effects on the unborn child.

Researchers have found that mothers who smoke during pregnancy may be more likely to bear smaller babies. This is a concern because small newborns, usually those weighing less than 2.1kgs, tend to be at risk for a variety of problems, including learning disorders. Alcohol also may be dangerous to the foetus' developing brain. It appears that alcohol may distort the developing neurons.

Heavy alcohol use during pregnancy has been linked to foetal alcohol syndrome, a condition that can lead to low birth weight, intellectual impairment, hyperactivity, and certain physical defects. Any alcohol use during pregnancy, however, may influence the child's development and lead to problems with learning, attention, memory, or problem solving. Because scientists have not yet identified "safe" levels, alcohol should be used cautiously by women who are pregnant or who may soon become pregnant.

Drugs:

Such as cocaine--especially in its smokable form seems to affect the normal development of brain receptors. These brain cell parts help to transmit incoming signals from our skin, eyes, and ears, and help regulate our physical response to the environment. Because children with certain learning disabilities have difficulty understanding speech sounds or letters, some researchers believe that learning disabilities, as well as ADHD, may be related to faulty receptors. Current research points to drug abuse as a possible cause of receptor damage.

Problems during Pregnancy or Delivery:

Other possible causes of learning disabilities involve complications during pregnancy. In some cases, the mother's immune system reacts to the foetus and attacks it as if it were an infection. This type of disruption seems to cause newly formed brain cells to settle in the wrong part of the brain. Or during delivery, the umbilical cord may become twisted and temporarily cut off oxygen to the foetus. This, too, can impair brain functions and lead to LD.

In addition, there is growing evidence that learning problems may develop in children with cancer who had been treated with chemotherapy or radiation at an early age. This seems particularly true of children with brain tumours who received radiation to the skull.

Section 4:

Emotional Burden....

Understand Them...

ANXIETY

Anxiety is the most frequent emotional symptom reported by Dyslexic adults. Dyslexic children are more fearful in nature because of their constant frustration and confusion in school. These feelings are exacerbated by the unpredictable and inconsistent pattern of dyslexia. You might close encounters where kids would have episodes of anticipated failure. I have experienced arenas where new situations can become a fresh source of anxiety.

Anxiety causes human beings to avoid whatever frightens them. The dyslexic child is no exception. The problem arises when parents, guardians and teachers fail to understand symptoms and misinterpret the child's reluctance or evasive behaviour as indifference or laziness. When the dyslexic child avoids homework or anything to do with reading and writing, it is not because they don't want to but because the hesitancy to participate in school is related more to anxiety and confusion than to apathy.

ANGER

Many of the emotional problems caused by dyslexia occur out of frustration with school or social situations. Psychologists have frequently observed that frustration produces anger. Which can be clearly witnessed in every individual; Bear in mind what a child who doesn't understand why he/she can't perform like other kids in school feel.

Anger is an emotion clearly visible in a child who is dyslexic. The reason behind their anger is often the school work writing assignments and reactions from parents and teachers. That is when you find them looking out for venues to vent their anger and the easy target would be the sibling or the parent. Mothers are particularly likely to feel the dyslexic's wrath.

Very often, the dyslexic child sits through these feelings in school and regardless of the surrounding becomes very passive. Once in their comfort zone, which could be home or the company of someone with whom they are comfortable, these feelings erupt like a volcano directing the anger towards the individual around them.

It is the child's trust on that one individual that allows him to vent his anger. This scenario though cannot be justified as the individual in contact with the child's feelings tends to feel frustrated and confused while they are desperately trying to help their child.

As youngsters reach adolescence, society expects them to become independent. The tension between the expectation of independence and the child's learned dependence causes great internal conflicts. The adolescent dyslexic uses his anger to break away from those people whom he feel he is dependent on.

Because of these factors, it may be difficult for parents, guardians or teachers to help their teenage dyslexic. This is when you will find them constantly trying to bond with a older sibling or a peer and letting them intervene at this age helps the child more.

SELF - IMAGE

The dyslexic child's self–image appears to be extremely vulnerable to frustration and anxiety. According to Erik Erikson, a German-born American developmental psychologist and psychoanalyst known for his theory on psychosocial development of human beings, most famous for coining the phrase *"IDENTITY CRISIS"*, explains that during the first years of school, every child must resolve the conflicts between a positive self–image and feelings of inferiority. If children succeed in school, they will develop positive feelings about themselves and believe that they can succeed in life.

If children meet failure and frustration, they learn that they are inferior to others, and that their effort makes very little difference. Instead of feeling powerful and productive, they learn that their environment controls them. They feel powerless and incompetent, paving way towards an identity crisis. Researchers have learned that when typical learners succeed, they credit their own efforts for their success. When they fail, they tell themselves to try harder. However, when the dyslexic succeeds, he is likely to attribute his success to luck. When he fails, he simply sees himself as stupid. I have personally experienced this too. I have had my child come home to tell me, "Mom I got lucky today! I got a star in my math assignment!"

Early intervention of these feelings would help a great deal. Mainly when you explain to them that these feelings are normal and that though people could get lucky his/her grades were purely due to hard-work and not luck.

Research also suggests that these feelings of inferiority develop by the age of ten. After this age, it becomes extremely difficult to help the child develop a positive self–image.

DEPRESSION:

Depression is also a frequent complication in dyslexia. Although most dyslexics are not depressed, children with this
kind of learning disability are at higher risk for intense feelings of sorrow and pain. Perhaps because of their low self–esteem, dyslexics are afraid to turn their anger toward their environment and instead turn it toward themselves.

Depressed children and adolescents would have different symptoms when compared to a depressed adult. You would never find a depressed child behaving lethargic nor would they talk about their feelings. Hyper active, destructive, physical abusive, verbal abuse would be their way of covering up their inner feelings or emotional pain. Masking depression, the child may not seem to portray obvious unhappiness. Children who are depressed tend to have three common characteristics:

- First, they tend to have negative thoughts about themselves, i.e. a negative self–image.
- Second, they tend to view the world negatively. They are less likely to enjoy the positive experiences in life making it difficult for them to have fun.

- Finally, most depressed children have great trouble imagining anything positive about the future or experience anything that's beautiful. The depressed dyslexic not only experiences great pain in his present experiences, but also foresees a life of continuing failure.

FAMILY TURMOIL:

Similar to any condition that embarks handicapped scenarios, dyslexia has a tremendous impact on the child's family. Unlike other physical ailment which is visible, dyslexia is an invisible,
and these effects are often overlooked.

Sibling rivalry is the most common factor that the family sees itself being effected in. Siblings who are non–dyslexic often feel a pang of jealousy towards the dyslexic child, who gets the majority of the parents' attention, time, and money.

On the contrary, the dyslexic child hates the attention and just wishes to be left alone, increasing the chances of negative behaviour and detests the achieving child in the family.

Section 5:

WHY IS IT DISCOURAGING AND FRUSTRATING TO BE DYSLEXIC!!!

The frustration of children with dyslexia often revolves on their inability to meet expectations of parents, guardians and teachers. They see a bright, enthusiastic child who is not learning to read and write. Time and again, dyslexics and their parents hear, "He's such a bright child; if only he would try harder." On the contrary, no one knows exactly how hard the dyslexic is trying.

The feeling of guilt and remorse which builds within them because they fail to meet other people's expectations is overruled only by a dyslexics' inability to achieve their goals. There are kids who tend to develop a perfectionists attitude in order to deal with anxiety. They grow up believing that it is "terrible" to make a mistake if they are surrounded by people who seem not to understand or just tend to overlook the cause of underperformance.

Their learning disability, true to its' definition means that these children will make many "careless" or "stupid" mistakes. This can be a cause of extreme frustration, making the feel persistently inadequate or a perfect subject to failure.

The dyslexic frequently has problems with social relationships. These can be traced to causes:

- Dyslexic children may be physically and socially immature in comparison to their peers. This can lead to a poor self-image and less peer acceptance.
- Dyslexics' social immaturity may make them awkward in social situations.

- Many dyslexics have difficulty reading social cues. They may be oblivious to the amount of personal distance necessary in social interactions or insensitive to other people's body language.
- Dyslexia often affects oral language functioning. Affected children may have trouble finding the right words, may stammer, or may pause before answering direct questions. This puts them at a disadvantage as they enter adolescence, when language becomes more central to their relationships.
- Observations by clinical psychologists and psychiatrists prove that dyslexics have difficulty in not only remembering the sequence of letters or words, but can also have difficulty remembering the order of events.
  - For instance, an interaction between two children; A dyslexic child might ride another child's bicycle. The child who owns the bicycle may throw a tantrum (they are kids after all!) This would directly lead to a fight, and eventually lands in a bout of physical fight! The Dyslexic child when relating to the experience might reverse the sequence of events. He may remember that the other child called him a name or picked a physical fight because of which he took the bicycle and hit the other child.

One, the child finds it difficult to sequence the scene. Two, they has trouble learning from their mistakes. Three, if an adult or a peer who happened to be witness confronts, they look like they are lying.

Interactions between children involve not the superficial visible events but many more underlying events. Considering the child's sequencing and memory problems, the dyslexic may relate a different sequence of events each time he tells the tale. Parents, guardians and teachers, end up assuming that the child is a pathological liar.

Inconsistencies of this condition produce serious challenges in a child's life. Every child whether dyslexic or normal has a variable degree in their own individual ability. But, a dyslexic child's ability is greatly exaggerated. Their strengths and weakness could be vastly inter-related.

I came across a dyslexic adult who could play with numbers and could solve any complex problem. Ask him to remember names and numbers and it would be a problem. "I have heard him say there is something wrong with me! I just can't remember!"

These fluctuations in understanding and moods typically create a whirlpool of emotions and effects in a dyslexic child. They constantly find themselves in paradigms where they can accomplish tasks with ease where the peers are unable to finish or find it very taxing and immediately encounter tasks that are simple and easy to everyone but they complete them with utmost difficulty or sometimes go unfinished. One discussion with a dyslexic adult resulted in me coming to terms with a new terminology. "I felt I was walking into a dark basement with no ventilation or light!"

As a mother I felt I had to ensure that my child never came back to me with these feelings of despair or loss of hope. I felt I had to educate my child with the kind of problems that could arise and also provide sufficient backup to help equip better in these scenarios. To deal with these kinds of problems, dyslexics need a thorough understanding of their learning disability. This will help them predict both success and failure. Dyslexics also perform erratically within tasks.

The errors they commit are pretty inconsistent. Ask a dyslexic child to write a paragraph and you would find a word spelled in different ways. Once, while playing a word game, asked a dyslexic child to spell the word television on multiple occasions randomly. Every time the word was given an entirely new spelling. This type of variation makes remediation more difficult.

The dyslexics' performance varies from day to day. You will find some interesting variations in their day to day activities. On certain, reading may come fairly easily and the same passage that they read with ease earlier would take an effort to the next day.
The point to be noted here is that this inconsistency in their reading patterns, are extremely confusing not only to the dyslexic, but also to others associating with them.

The dyslexics, performance fluctuates. This makes it extremely difficult for the child to learn to compensate, because he or she cannot predict the intensity of the symptoms on a given day.

Section 6:

SWIM THE WAVES

Parents of young children and professionals working with young children watch with anticipation the developmental milestones indicating a child is picking up the skills expected at a certain age. In the first year of life that focus is typically on motor skills, in the second year attention shifts to language development.

Specific developmental dyslexia runs in families. This means that one or both of the child's parents may have had similar school problems. When faced with a child who is having school problems, dyslexic parents may react in one of two ways. They may deny the existence of dyslexia and believe if the child would just buckle down, he or she could succeed. Or, the parents may relive their failures and frustrations through their child's school experience. This brings back powerful and terrifying emotions, which can interfere with the adult's parenting skills.

The development of communication through language is an instinctive process. Language is our most common means of interacting with one another, and children begin the process naturally.
Neurobiologist Dr. Lise Eliot writes: "the reason language is instinctive is because it is, to a large extent, hard-wired in the brain.

Just as we evolve neural circuits for eating and seeing, so has our brain, together with a sophisticated vocal apparatus, evolved a complex neural circuit for rapidly perceiving, analyzing, composing, and producing language" (Eliot, 1999).

We also know, however, that the experiences provided in a child's environment are critical for the development of language. It is this interplay of nature and nurtures that result in our ability to communicate, but the process of learning language begins with how the brain is structured.

The brain is structured for language. Neuroscientists tell us that a baby is born with millions of brain cells, all he or she will ever need. Each brain cell has branching appendages, called dendrites, which reach out to make connections with other brain cells. The places where brain cells connect are called synapses. When electrical signals pass from brain cell to brain cell, they cross the synapse between the cells.

When synapses are stimulated over and over, that pattern of neural connections is "hard-wired" in the brain. It becomes an efficient, permanent pathway that allows signals to be transmitted quickly and accurately. Advances in brain-imaging technology in recent years have confirmed this process.

New technology has allowed us to see that there are physical differences in a child's brain that has been appropriately stimulated, versus one that has suffered lack of stimulation. Connections that are not stimulated by repeated experiences atrophy, or fade away. It is truly a "use-it-or-lose-it" situation.

We know that reorganization of the connections between brain cells after birth is highly impacted by experiences provided by the child's environment.

Parents play an invaluable role in influencing the child's cognitive, language, motor, and social emotional development. It is through providing repeated, positive experiences for their child that parents have a lasting impact on his or her child's brain development.

Critical periods in brain development accommodate the development of specific skills, language being one of these. During certain times in the child's life, the brain is active in forming connections for specific abilities.

While critical periods are prime times for the development of specific neural synapses, skills can still be learned after a window of opportunity has closed, but with greater time and effort. It is during these critical periods that lack of stimulation or negative experiences can have the most impact.

Parents can support their child's brain development for language during these times by providing experiences that allow the child to practice emerging skills. Opportunities during the course of the day to engage in face-to-face interaction, hear language being spoken, listen to the written word read aloud, and practice associating objects with words provide language experiences without undue stress or overstimulation.

While a new-born does not use words, he/she is definitely able to communicate. He/she can look into his father's or mother's
face in a way that tells them he wants to hear their voices. By crying he is able to let them know when he is hungry, cold, needs a diaper change, or has other needs to be met.

An infant's brain responds best to a type of speech called "parentese," which adults use naturally when speaking to babies. Parentese uses short, simple sentences, prolonged vowel sounds, more inflection in the voice, and a higher pitch than the speech used when talking to another adult. Studies have shown that when parents spoke parentese, the baby was able to connect words sooner to the objects they represent.

Brain development information simply reinforces much of what early childhood experts have been suggesting for years. The development of language is tremendously influenced by parent-child interactions.

In the first year, it is important to talk, sing, and read to the baby often so he can learn the sounds of his native language. In addition to learning the sounds of speech, during the first six months a child's brain begins to learn which mouth movements go with the sounds. That is the reason it is important to have lots of face-to-face conversations with the baby as the parent interprets the world around him/her.

Cooing, and then babbling are milestones in language acquisition. Babies like to mimic what they hear. By speaking to the child and imitating the child's sounds, a parent not only teaches the child sound patterns but encourages taking turns, a process necessary for conversation.

Studies have shown that children whose parents spoke to them more often know many more words by age two and scored higher on standardized tests by age three than those whose parents did not.

In the second year of life, the brain organizes the connections for language when the child sees pictures in a book and hears the parent give names for the pictures simultaneously.

Parents and other primary caregivers can help language development at this age by reciting nursery rhymes, songs, and poems throughout the day. Activities such as using a mirror to point out and name facial features are also helpful at this age. Ideal times for story-telling and reading are quiet, relaxed moments before naptime or bedtime.

Between 24 and 35 months of age the brain is getting better at forming mental symbols for objects, people, and events. This is directly related to the growing ability to use many more words and short sentences.

Delays in language can have a variety of sources. When parents suspect such delays it is always prudent to check with a professional. Repeated ear infections in the first few years delay expressive language.

It is always important to watch for signs of ear infections in a young child, such as not reacting to sound, pulling one's ears, reluctance to suck, resistance to laying down, or having an upper respiratory infection.

Speaking two languages at home:
Hearing two languages spoken at home is a real advantage to the child. If a child hears two languages from birth, he or she will maintain the ability to hear the sounds of both and be able to speak each language with the accent of a native speaker.

If parents each speak a different language, it is helpful if the child hears the same language consistently from the parent who is its native speaker. If, for example, the mother is a native English speaker and the father a native Spanish speaker, it will be less confusing for the child to hear each parent speak in his or her native language.

The child may mix the languages in his or her own speech initially, but will typically sort it out by approximately two and one-half years of age. Then he or she will separate the words belonging to each language and know which language to use with which parent. By seven years of age, the child is likely to be able to cope with the two language systems without a problem, using both vocabulary and grammar appropriate for his age.

If a child enters a pre-school and is first exposed to a second language after the age of three, she will still be able to acquire the second language easily because she knows the rules of communication. In three to seven months the child will begin to understand the second language. After about two years she will be able to carry-on a fluent conversation.

Young children learn a second language more easily than adults because the window of opportunity for learning language is still open for them. Helping the child build her self-confidence during the time she is learning a second language is very important.

Music is a great way to help the child learn words and phrases in the new language. Talking slowly, clearly, and simply is also helpful. It is also important for parents to continue speaking to the child at home in their native language because it continues to lay the foundation for the second language by providing the basic rules of communication. Also, the parent-child interaction might suffer if the parents speak less to the child in an attempt to use the second language.

HELP THEM READ:

They might read for pleasure, or you could read to them for pleasure. Say a story book a comic or a newspaper. You can read at your own pace and it doesn't matter whether they know all the words, or remember all the details.

Reading for study, is another story. It is important to get the facts right, to remember the relevant information and understand what the writer is saying. If you see that your child has a lot of material to read it makes sense to:

- Get them comfortable – have the right light and a quiet place.
- Have pencils, highlighters, notebooks and any other aids you need to hand.
- If you feel they need reference books or dictionaries have them on their desk as searching for materials damages their concentration and focus span.

- Never let them sit down to read a book or document without asking them just why they are reading and what information they want to get.
- Skim through, looking at chapter headings and summaries.
- Help them look for the key ideas and underline with pencil or highlighter.
- Stop from time to time and ask them what they have just read.
- Let them read for 20 – 30 minutes and then take a short break. It is difficult to concentrate effectively for more than 30 minutes without a break.
- Help them review what they you have read by making them come up with their own short summary.
- Role play with them like they are giving a talk on what they have read.
- Check back to make sure that they have got all facts right.

There is a well-known method for reading which explains and covers the above tips and it is easy to remember because it is called **SQ3R**. This method, which was first developed by Francis Robinson in the 1960s, has been used for many years.

- **S – SCAN**
    - Look through the text quickly for key words, not ignoring any illustrations, diagrams or graphs Important information is often highlighted in a text box or in bold or italics.

- **Q – QUESTIONING**
    - Ask yourself what information you hope to get from your reading.

- **3R – READ, REMEMBER, REVIEW**
    - Read – read the text fully.
    - Remember – write down the main points.
    - Review – read again to check if you have remembered correctly.

If you need to add an extra edge on helping your child remember what they have read in great detail, say for an examination, it may help to read aloud and tape the material. I personally find this very effective. It can be replayed as often as they like at any convenient time. If you find that they read quite easily but still have problems with new or uncommon words, it might be worthwhile teaching them to chunk information in smaller pieces.

HELP THEM WRITE:

Next to reading aloud, writing is probably the activity most disliked by kids with dyslexia. Even when the writing load would seem to be a minor part of the work load, it can make life very difficult. Dyslexia is considered a language based learning disorder and is thought of as a reading disability but it also impacts a student's ability to write. There is often a large discrepancy between what a student thinks and can tell you orally and what he can write down on paper. Besides frequent spelling errors, some of the ways dyslexia affects writing skills:

- Essays are written as one paragraph with several long, run-on sentences.
- Using little punctuation, including not capitalizing the first word in a sentence or using end punctuation.
- Odd or no spacing between words.
- Cramming information on the page rather than spreading out.

In addition, many students with dyslexia show signs of dysgraphia; including having illegible handwriting and taking a long time to form letters and write assignments. As with reading, students with dyslexia spend so much time and effort writing the words, the meaning behind the words can be lost. Added to difficulties in organizing and sequencing information, writing paragraphs, essays and reports is time consuming and frustrating.

Kids may jump around when writing, with events occurring out of sequence. Because not all children with dyslexia have the same level of symptoms, writing problems can be hard to spot. While some may only have minor problems, others would have handwritings that are impossible to read and understand.

Grammar and Writing Skills:

Dyslexic kids put much effort into reading individual words and trying to understand the meanings behind the words. Grammar and writing skills, to them, may not seem important. But without grammar skills, writing doesn't always make sense.

You as a parent can take extra time to teach conventions, such as standard punctuation, what constitutes a sentence fragment, how to avoid run-on sentences and capitalization. Although this may be an area of weakness, focusing on grammar rules helps. Give kids time to practice and master these skills before moving on to additional skills. I have personally experienced that speaking in English at home helps the kids with the communicative ability.

Dysgraphia, also known as written expression disorder, is a neurological learning disability that often accompanies dyslexia. Students with dysgraphia have poor or illegible handwriting.

Many children with dysgraphia also have sequencing difficulties. Besides poor handwriting and sequencing skills, symptoms include:

- Grammar and spelling errors
- Inconsistencies in written assignments, such as different size letters, mix of cursive and print writing, letters with different slants
- Omitting letters and words
- Non-existent spacing between words and sentences and cramming the words on the paper
- Unusual grip of pencil or pen

Kids with dysgraphia can often write neatly, but this takes an enormous amount of time and effort. They take time to form each letter and will often miss the meaning of what they are writing because their focus is on forming each individual letter.

As a parent you can help your child improve their writing skills by working together to edit and make corrections in their written work. Writing to them would prove more of a punishment than pleasure. I have had experiences of my kid falling asleep in less than 3mins when asked to write. I have noticed that when asked to read a pictorial book (which helps them create and frame sentences) he always read what he meant to write or meant to say than what is actually printed. Having them orally read the written assignment back can help you as a parent in understanding what they meant.

The most important factor to keep in mind while your child writes is to ensure that they do not get not to get bogged down in one part. As you find your child struggling or getting stuck at an area help them move to another topic and bring them back to this as and when you find them less stressed. Check carefully from time to time that you are helping them stick to the topic and not going off into other arenas.

Letting the kid's use the laptop or the desktop to write also helps. If your computer has a facility for converting text to voice, use this to edit their written work. For those with a good ear, it is easier to detect mistakes when you hear them, than when you read from the screen or the paper. Take extra care with words like 'their' for 'there' or 'wait' for 'weight'.

Sometimes dyslexic kids place too much pressure on themselves to have perfect spelling. It helps a great deal to let them know that everyone makes mistakes when writing or typing, not just people with dyslexia!

HELP THEM MEMORISE:

It is often said that with dyslexia it is not so much that kids learn slowly but that they forget quickly. It is true that kids with dyslexia often struggle to remember names, dates, and facts. Stress and anxiety can make this difficulty worse. Most kids will recall the panic they felt as a child being asked a question in mental arithmetic, or spelling when an immediate response was required. The greater the effort, the further away the answer drifts.

Memory is a very complex area in a dyslexic child. The central features of the dyslexic profile, such as issues with concentration and short-term memory recall, the proposition here, is the one biggest single issue that kids with dyslexia have to deal with! ANXIETY DUE TO LOSS IN MEMORY!!!

Anxiety is not in itself a bad thing. If there is too little, there is no motive to act. If there is too much, there is paralysis, and this is where it becomes problematic. What distinguishes the kids is the intensity; this 'too much' that is debilitating and prevents the child from being able to function effectively or sometimes function at all.

What brings about this 'too much' is trauma and its source can be spectacular or obscure. Trauma here is something that doesn't even occur to the child's intellect or inner-self. When you find the behavioural patterns of aggression, its' important to understand that the child here hardly has a clue of what's happening. When they do recover, the recovery time and span is varied. Here I would like to call this feeling as falling apart.

We see the effects of this 'falling apart' in the range of symptoms present in dyslexia, Mental blocks; problems with concentration and short-term memory; panic; the disorientation manifest in the translation of ideas into 3D space, such as: text doesn't make sense to others, issues with structure and layout, and arguments being 'all over the place'.

These are the symptoms that are present in any mind that is at the end of its threshold. Children with dyslexia relate and attribute to these challenges that are beyond their knowledge. The inconsistent and incomplete, realisation of their own lack of ability to know and analyse situations; Overwhelming the child with the feeling that they should have been prepared or must understand their state triggers anxiety!

If it is handed down as if the child should already know, this will act as a trigger to anxiety. The situation being presented as if its' a task in progress creates a more assimilable atmosphere around the child.

Children with dyslexia cannot accept propositions at face value, as they are concerned with the truth value of knowledge. It is very important to understand how knowledge is delivered. The validity of propositions has to be tested against experience before they can be used. Children without learning difficulties are usually not concerned with the truth value of propositions in an absolute sense, and so can be tactical in their study. But, a child with a learning disorder needs to be explained and given details of the why and how.

Short-term memory gets a bad press. It functions as an interface between the subject and the outside world, prioritising the demands that are placed on him/her, precisely determining what is most important to the subject, to act on this and forget the rest.

Children with dyslexia normally have difficulty with saying 'no' to demands placed on them. The consequences of forgetting are usually relatively trivial, whereas the consequences of not being able to forget are potentially devastating.

A close look into why a child with dyslexia forgets often or taking the efforts to draw the patterns of their forgetful nature will etch out the understanding that he/she uses "I FORGOT!" as a safety valve to prevent overload!

De facto, its' the want to be able to say 'NO!' in the first place that sketches out an "I FORGOT!"

Commonly, memory enhancing techniques are recommended in response to this. While these are useful, the subject needs to be alerted to this way of interpreting limits in short-term memory.
Further, the development of time management and organisation skills enable better decisions regarding the feasibility of taking on commitments at any one time, as well as increasing the capacity to multi-task.

Dyslexia can be read as an 'anxiety disorder', although it is also a way of reducing and treating that anxiety through symptoms such as short-term memory 'deficits' and concentration drift, failing examinations and limiting intellectual achievement.

The effect of an outbreak of anxiety, however subtle, is that the child bails out of the problem-solving process (loss of concentration) before they have a real chance of completing it. The repetition of this experience reinforces a pre-existing belief that they are not capable of completing the task.

Technological support systems and adjustments in school life offered to children with the vision of wanting to provide shortcuts through study tasks gradually extend the time that the child is able to persevere in the task and so discover that it is, indeed, possible to be able to finish an assignment or a task on hand.
Learning support aimed at developing thinking skills and strategizing techniques prove very helpful.

Children can ask questions and find the missing links that previously made it impossible for them to use particular concepts. Developing abstract skills that come into play without the child even being aware of them works better, as the child doesn't feel the pressure of studying or learning!

Where anxiety is explicit, panic attacks around examinations or submission deadlines, children should be referred to the counselling services within the school or be taken to a psychological counsellor. A mother proves a better source of confidence to the child, provided the child and parent are on a comfortable wavelength.

Giving them the confidence enables them to speak about that which is nonsensical, that which erupts into the centre of their work and blots out the possibility of understanding by giving this non-sense a place and a value, it helps a great deal for the child to understand and feel ok about the situation. It does not have to present as a disruption to other activity to the same extent.

In the longer term speaking about what distresses them enables the child to increasingly take their feeling into control, rather than being 'swayed' by what other people have to say, which has to be second. It works to construct a positioning.

Interestingly, memory is very complex and we have different memory ability for different stimuli. Some people with dyslexia have very good visual memory and poor auditory memory, so they will remember information better if it is presented with diagrams and visual images. Other people with dyslexia may have poor visual memory and good auditory memory, so they will find it easier to remember what they hear, rather than what they see.

People who are more kinaesthetic or active learners will remember better by practicing and doing an activity, rather than just reading about it or looking at it. There are two main types of memory relating to the length of recall, but for facts and figures we usually need two in particular: short-term and long-term. Short-term memory is used when you hold a fact, say a phone number, in your head long enough to use it. By the following day, you no longer recall it, or need to recall it.

PERORATION

The effects of learning disabilities can ripple outward from the disabled child or adult to family, friends, and peers at school or work.

Children with LD often absorb what others thoughtlessly say about them. They may define themselves in light of their disabilities, as "behind," "slow," or "different."

Sometimes they don't know how they're different, but they know how awful they feel. Their tension or shame can lead them to act out in various ways--from withdrawal to belligerence. Many may get into fights. They may stop trying to learn and achieve and eventually drop out of school. They may become isolated and depressed.

Children with learning disabilities and attention disorders may have trouble making friends with peers. Children with delays may be more comfortable with younger children who play at their level.

Without professional help, the situation can spiral out of control. The more children or teenagers fail, the more they may act out their frustration and damage their self-esteem. The more they act out, the more trouble and punishment it brings, further lowering their self-esteem. Children who lashed out when teased about their poor pronunciation could get repeatedly punished in school.

Having a child with a learning disability may also be an emotional burden for the family. Parents often sweep through a range of emotions: denial, guilt, blame, frustration, anger, and despair. Brothers and sisters may be annoyed or embarrassed by their sibling, or jealous of all the attention the child with LD gets.

Counselling can be very helpful to people with LD and their families. Counselling can help affected children, teenagers, and adults develop greater self-control and a more positive attitude toward their own abilities. Talking with a counsellor or psychologist also allows family members to air their feelings as well as get support and reassurance.

Behaviour modification also seems to help many children with LD. In behaviour modification, children receive immediate, tangible rewards when they act appropriately. Receiving an immediate reward can help children learn to control their own actions, both at home and in class. A school or private counsellor can explain behaviour modification and help parents and teachers set up appropriate rewards for the child.

Parents and teachers can help by structuring tasks and environments for the child in ways that allow the child to succeed. They can find ways to help children build on their strengths and work around their disabilities. This may mean deliberately making eye contact before speaking to a child with an attention disorder.

For a teenager with a language problem, it may mean providing pictures and diagrams for performing a task. Children with handwriting or spelling problems, a solution may be to provide a word processor and software that checks spelling. A counsellor or school psychologist can help identify practical solutions that make it easier for the child and family to cope day by day.

Every child needs to grow up feeling competent and loved. When children have learning disabilities, parents may need to work harder at developing their children's self-esteem and relationship-building skills. I believe self-esteem and good relationships are as far more worthy than just plain academic skills.

Sources of Information

Several publications help individuals, teachers, and families to understand and cope with learning disabilities. The following resources provide a good starting point for gaining insight, practical solutions, and support. Further information can be found at book stores.

Publications
- Books for Children and Teens With Learning Disabilities
- The Survival Guide for Kids
- Learning Disabilities and the Don't-Give-Up-Kid.
- Different, Not Dumb.
- Keeping A Head in School: A Student's Book about Learning Abilities and Learning Disorders.

Books for Adults With Learning Disabilities

- Adelman, P., and Wren, C. Learning Disabilities, Graduate School, and Careers: The Student's Perspective.
- Cordoni, B. Living with a Learning Disability.
- Kravets, M., and Wax, I. The K&W Guide: Colleges and the Learning Disabled Student.

Books for Parents

- Greene, L. Learning Disabilities and Your Child: A Survival Handbook.
- Novick, B., and Arnold, M. Why Is My Child Having Trouble in School?
- Silver, L. The Misunderstood Child: A Guide for Parents of Children with Learning Disabilities
- Silver, L. Dr. Silver's Advice to Parents on Attention-Deficit Hyperactivity Disorder.
- Vail, P. Smart Kids with School Problems.
- Weiss, E. Mothers Talk About Learning Disabilities.

Books and Pamphlets for Teachers and Specialists

- Adelman, P., and Wren, C. Learning Disabilities, Graduate School, and Careers.
- Silver, L. ADHD: Attention Deficit-Hyperactivity Disorder, Booklet for Teachers.
- Smith, S. Success Against the Odds: Strategies and Insights from the Learning Disabled.
- Wender, P. The Hyperactive Child, Adolescent, and Adult. Attention Disorder